Free Verse Editions
Edited by Jon Thompson

# A MYTH OF ARIADNE

Martha Ronk

Winner of the New Measure Poetry Prize

Parlor Press
Anderson, South Carolina
www.parlorpress.com

Parlor Press LLC, Anderson, South Carolina, 29621


Printed in the United States of America
S A N: 2 5 4 - 8 8 7 9

Library of Congress Cataloging-in-Publication Data on File

Names: Ronk, Martha Clare, author.
Title: A myth of Ariadne / Martha Ronk.
Description: Anderson, South Carolina : Parlor Press, [2022] | Series: Free verse editions | Summary: "The poems address De Chirico's Ariadne paintings: the myth and then the particular way De Chirico presents Ariadne as a sexualized statue threatened by intrusions of locomotives, ships, shadows, conspirators"-- Provided by publisher.
Identifiers: LCCN 2021044176 (print) | LCCN 2021044177 (ebook) | ISBN 9781643172859 (paperback) | ISBN 9781643172866 (pdf) | ISBN 9781643172873 (epub)
Subjects: LCGFT: Poetry.
Classification: LCC PS3568.O574 M98 2022 (print) | LCC PS3568.O574 (ebook) | DDC 811/.54--dc23
LC record available at https://lccn.loc.gov/2021044176
LC ebook record available at https://lccn.loc.gov/2021044177

978-1-64317-285-9 (paperback)
978-1-64317-286-6 (pdf)
978-1-64317-287-3 (ePub)

1 2 3 4 5


Cover design by David Blakesley.

Parlor Press, LLC is an independent publisher of scholarly and trade titles in print and multimedia formats. This book is available in paperback and ebook formats from Parlor Press on the World Wide Web at http://www.parlorpress.com or through online and brick-and-mortar bookstores. For submission information or to find out about Parlor Press publications, write to Parlor Press, 3015 Brackenberry Drive, Anderson, South Carolina, 29621, or email editor@parlorpress.com.

## Contents

# Preface

The poems address De Chirico's Ariadne series of paintings preceding World War I: the myth and then the particular way De Chirico presents Ariadne as a statue threatened by intrusions of distant locomotives, ships, lengthening shadows, seeming conspirators. I see the statue of Ariadne as evidence for the ways in which we turn aside from atrocity and loss (she sleeping in the aftermath of her encounter with the Minotaur and her abandonment by Theseus) into numbing forgetfulness. Despite her presence as a statue in the paintings, she also appears as an exposed body, a sexualized object always under threat.

My series, like his series, depends on the technique of disjunction. Like his, my series rests on anxiety punctuated by images of violence, the seductive pleasures of forgetfulness, and exists in the space between the paintings, De Chirico's memoir and poems, and a jangled depiction of a woman's history.

*What is especially needed is great sensitivity to look upon everything in the world as enigma. . . To live in the world as in an immense museum of strange things.*

—de Chirico (MOMA introduction)

*The body is understood to be an active process of embodying certain cultural and historical possibilities, a complicated process of appropriation which any phenomenological theory of embodiment needs to describe. In order to describe the gendered body, a phenomenological theory of constitution requires an expansion of the conventional view of acts to mean both that which constitutes meaning and that through which meaning is performed or enacted.*

—Judith Butler

# The Labyrinth

She let the hero find his way with her thread
the ends of her knitting needles, her errancy.
Then she slept again in a deep blue color.

The locomotive noses into her open air bedroom
the sails of the ship flap off shore
and a palm tree opens up for the blowing stars.

This is the rhythm of a life collecting in the cells
and blood aches with knowing something about the end of the story
something about the monster she carried around with her for years.

The gauzy marble blouse clings to her skin in the endless heat.

## *The Soothsayer's Recompense*, 1913

She seems to be rolling off the edge of her plinth—
all it would take is one elbow more or less, one knee opening
and she'll fall onto the sandy expanse.
It's late in the day, shadows deepening toward evening
and the clock reads just before 2.
Detached from any building, an arch frames tilted palms
blown by a certain predictable wind.
A pencil sketch from June mapped out the composition
shifting perspective at the base of the statue.
There is no way I could have known how it would turn out
as we lay in our bathing suits on the sand as the sun tipped
toward evening and looking like the ghostly children we were.

## A girl running (and *Mystery and Melancholy of a Street)*

*We wanted the war to be over; but once wars start they seem never to finish, just like the tragedies and suffering they cause.*

—De Chirico

Arches puncture the white arcade, blackened despite light that whitens
as it descends, blasts into incised shadow—flattened cutouts emerge,
buildings slip from their concrete and lower below the threshold,
we've crossed the divide between one ochre and another, a trauma
no child can comprehend, as side-stepping the openings of arches and
    carriage wheels,
the girl's running in the windowdressing of sunlight,
while the soldier stands ominously silent at the end of the diagonal,
raising the inevitable shadow lance.

## *Melanconia* 191

> *It was after a long intestinal illness when I looked out*
> *on the streets I had seen many times before.*
>
> —De Chirico

The piazza seems in its vast expanse to be convalescent.
It hangs waiting for war.
It extends and extends as if there were a cause
behind the proclamations and arcades.
Over there on the far wall apples and pears eaten in about 1913,
framed, off-white and raw.
In a long film they drove over miles of rubble.
On the front page a woman in a scarf threw a stone
at the oncoming tanks, her arm arched overhead as if it were just a ball,
the ends of her scarf blowing as she was moving before the camera
    caught her.
Afterwards the pieces settle, hands are put on the armrests
lifting and falling, belonging to someone else.

## Fetish

*What struck me most of all among the Ferrarese was a kind of more or less latent madness which could not escape an acute observer, such as I have always been. (gossipy etc.). Furthermore, the Ferrarese are also terribly lecherous; there are days, especially at the height of spring, in which the libidinous atmosphere which hangs over Ferrara becomes so strong that it can almost be heard, like the rushing water or the roar of fire . . . (fumes from hemp and perpetual humidity)*

—De Chirico

Each time he tried to make it the same as before,
each time he chose her name with A or took off her shoes.
Each time he wrapped her up in sheets and each time she
lay down to please him.
She wore the shoes but thought of them as missing like the book
she couldn't bring herself to read.
It made her edgy as if it were what they had been talking about.
In the distance was the wide wide world.
She tried to think of what it might be said to look like.
An open hole with multiple teeth, heels no one could walk in,
a Minotaur caught in chains and skins of hair.

## Objects from the story

The politician in marble is making a speech
while the boy tans himself by the base of the pedestal.
All the unnerving, all the skin, all at the same time.

Shadows larger than the predator's wings
strike across the muddy brown at so great a tilt the floor gives way.

One always knows it's coming closer despite
the bright turquoise wash behind the arcades, the boy's bony ribs.

Every object's too precise: the plant with dusty leaves,
the lines on the wooden planking, the box, as if on wheels,
sliding toward the oblivion of shadows.

## De Chirico's paints bought from Paciosi on via del Corso

The standard mixture of Dammar varnish,
linseed oil, and turpentine, dries too quickly and cracks,
flows erratically like estuaries where the arm of the sea
extends inland to meet the mouth, never mind how long
I stood looking at the legs of the trees
waiting for them to shift into the last time I stood
looking at them shifting imperceptibly to the left
as the neighbor gets into her car and admires her legs
getting in and shifting her weight into the position
of the driver and driving off having no stated destination,
discovering in words sufficient promptings, bespeaking distances themselves.
He would set it up and then you would begin to get
that murkiness flowing from the use of litharge
you had to use litharge in the right quantities and stand very still
you have to learn to stand absolutely still looking into the woods,
the coloration having shifted into "bilious, somber, measured,"
admiring the murkiness, the color of ponds dense with leaves.

## *The Enigma of the Hour* 1911

> *I became aware there is a host of strange things from*
> *the perspective of on-high.*
>
> —DeChirico

When he was laying plans no one could hear the execution.
He hands them over and makes time go by,
newspaper laid out in mosaic on the kitchen floornumbers rendered in muddy brown.
It might be minutes before three, standing apart as if they were draped in church cloth
as if there were anything to lean against, water spraying the desert air.
The bird with a ruddy breast is outside the window flapping.
The idea of flying overhead just to fly overhead,
the underside of a set of wings flat as newspaper sailing on the wind.

## Turin

When she sets the coffee to the side it spills over
the wooden chair, the man she's never seen before
who will show up later in the background.
Sometimes the man is wearing a small cap.
Sometimes he ponders a fountain.

She hears both men, distant as they are and she has no doubt
about what they are saying and what is arriving by the time
the story is slotted into place.

She has her eyes shut or else she can't stop to think what time it is
fixed at ten to three, what has happened to her already
helping the man who had lost his way between one ship and another,
lying out there exposed to the sun on the piazza of Turin

where Nietzsche succumbed to mental illness
after seeing a horse mercilessly flogged by a carriage driver in 1889.

## On the piazza, sounds

> *I had begun to paint subjects in which I tried to express the strong and mysterious feeling I had discovered in the books of Nietzsche: the melancholy of beautiful autumn days, afternoons in Italian cities. It was the prelude to the squares of Italy painted a little later in Paris and then in Milan, in Florence and in Rome.*
>
> —De Chirico

The melancholy of the beautiful is sheeting the day
as weather missing its music.
Her hands are over her eyes,
hoping to fend off sounds of explosions.

Mozart might be drifting over the piazza if she could hear
arias rolling off their tongues in the humid air.

We won't think about it, won't come near it.
The Piazza San Carlo stands alone in its sandy expanse
sun-drenched and but one of the causes.

*I saw that every angle of the palace,*
*every column, every window was an enigma.*
*A single bird sang in a cage.*

## *The Lassitude of the Infinite* c. 1913

She used to think of the future but she'd slept so long
she could think only of the weight of her own knees,
the vagaries of uneven thought, one resting slightly to the left of the other,
a weight she'd been given, the same story she said you always write.

Her sleep is like waking, she is listening to whatever is said
and the design of the ancient theater is to allow
the amplification of sound to reach all 3000 in the audience.
What is coming is always war, war against Thebes,
Afghanistan, and helicopters shot down over Hanoi.

At night she dreams the color of bruises, the sky she couldn't look into
before the story made it what it was. In diffusion, the mixing of
molecules as a result of Brownian motion, the mixing of blue ink through water,
the randomness by which she found herself lying on her side facing the wall.

## (departure

The light's as opaque as plaster
palm fronds fall in the street,
dust settles over the ochre lawn
the strict frame heightens sound
her elbows extend like a vapor of green she dreams of before she sleeps.
In the background the smooth line of horizon
marks the loosening day.      (Sail
But it's not the shift of seasons, not yet,
it's the shift of having waited not quite long enough,
there is more to come.

## The placement of the men shaking hands

You have to ask what are they doing
because although she is doing nothing,
they appear to be doing something just in their being together,
dressed as they are, suited-up and shaking hands
seems a conspiracy of sorts
because they are off to the side and in the shadows
it appears they are up to something.
At this point she has done what she meant to do and it is all over
but they appear to be getting back from an assignation of sorts,
from its starting all over again.

## *(light at midday strikes the piazza hard)*

Light comes straight down,
Her curses gather thick at noon.
In the painting the long shadows
encase the pain. She sees them first
as a muffled and rubbery sound.

She could tell by looking what was coming
in a long line of white cirrus
a shiver along the outside rim, a damp in the palm.
The story's been there all along
in the shadows growing longer in Turin.
To explain the effect of being so alone
as she was, intensively abandoned as she was,
extensively so.

*Tutte le case sono vuote*
*risucchiate dal cielo aspiratore.*
*Tutte le piazza deserte.*
*Tutti I piedistalli vedovi.*
*Le statue—emigrate in lunghe*
*caroane di pietra*
*verso porti lontani.*
*—Strane iscrizioni sorgono ad ogni quadrivio*
*Avvertimenti funebri di non andar più oltre—*

—De Chirico, *L'Ora Inquietante*

## *Sketch for 'Ariadne's Afternoon'* 1913

All you want to do is look in her face, its pale
place across from you, something misplaced about the lips.
Or if you take a walk to take it out of you and realize how severe
and unnecessary you've been all along.
Don't we all clamor for the undone and less,
the unravel at the base of the spine.
When I meant what I said. When it mattered not a whit.
The ache you used to like so much seems now pointless
and her face effortless and effete.
Taking the pencil and taking the edge off,
putting down whatever comes to mind,
decreasing the pressure of wrist to hand
making the barely perceptible, perceptibly there.

## A failing memory

She began to remember in random bits,
the years having gone in a habit of desultory reading,
couldn't any longer call up the entire system once so clear
and wasn't it the method of the rescue but she found herself
trying to see as a bird from overhead to get the lay of the land
the way the maze had been laid out and planned
but then after the wings and beak,
the hanging feet and bits of broken shell
and after thinking through the float itself
from its edges into the slightly moister center, she lost it
and though she knew the labyrinth had been somehow significant
it seemed to fade and she thought instead
she might have remembered how the sun hit the square
shadowed by the skeleton of a long-legged bird.

## The rectangular object

Eight years later eight paintings
and empathy.
The box in the corner, sorrows
in the angle of a street.
The object in one's own
shape and years.
The match of the inexact.
The dignity of rectangles, oneself bound
color and arch, within –as so rarely felt– one's own.
The dignity of rectangles, the open door
the lifted and lifting knee
the tangible shape of history.
The foreign heart (the slow hour) (the feet of marble) (a yellow plateau).

## Painting

They spoke then of sails and the varieties of talk.
The car door slams, everything is getting in the way.
It seems wind got her to thinking about fate.
It didn't seem much at the time, a small wind, some few lines,
whereas the exact length to which he goes to get
the length of the shadow across the ochre
is the length of the labyrinth out of which everything comes.
*In trauiger Stimmung* could be translated as:
the shadows grow longer in autumn
in Turin.

## A strange hour

She won't wake up. The others are talking about it and the steam is rising
under the arcade where she is what she is, an elbow, a sharp point of light.
She dreams the labyrinth of the ear but is now deaf marble.
She is slipping off the plinth as those of us at night relive falling,
draped figures moving closer to some of the vulnerable.
The paintings include outsized artichokes tipped on weighty sides,
include towers and shadows as if there were time in the face of a clock,
as if there were no manufacture or other shapes for the horrific.

*Due Carciofi di ferro sulla tavola d'ocra.*
*La geometria delle ombre staziava il cuore*
*al mattino immalinconichito.*

—De Chirico, *La Notte Misteriosa*

## The newspaper

I kept falling asleep in the part of the story where her lover left her

the flute repeating the phrase or repeating the sound of
canons going off one by one.

The overturned chess pieces mark out happenstance.

Once memory's lost
everything falls into illegible folds.

I try slack and easy gossip and wish for the dark days
when sleeping was a kind of respite.

I smooth the newspaper avoiding current reports of war.

I am hoping to shake hands warmly and with a full sense of attention.
How beautiful nevertheless the dark days, how wet my palms.

In this manner after several weeks the pile turns yellow
the pages stick and cannot be pried apart.

# Threads

*De Chirico began painting again in Paris, resuming the thread of Nietzschean inspiration*

For the mother most things led to cigarettes and fear.
Each thread she bit between her teeth and where are you going
she'd say as if we weren't attached.

Girls skipping with the edges of their dresses pinched
between finger and thumb, pinafores stitched in white.

She told him she loved the smell of nicotine on his fingers,
after she'd helped him find his way,
a slight whiff of hero, the threads of smoke around the bend,

her home by the lake and the full song as accompaniment
to the irresistible sound of the car.

## Newspaper accounts

All around the breakfast table they'd talk of it.
They'd walk out into the field in their thin suits and keep on.
Inside it was cool and no longer smelled of fried eggs, burned toast.
In there she knew what she wanted:
all of it played over again and no one ever missing.
She'd see water seeping away and coming in,
all the coffee in the world wouldn't wake her
all the estuaries turning inward in a slow slosh
feet wet from the tide coming in.
I'm too tired, she'd say, to think of him lost again
in the mazy fields, too tired to lift myself up.

## The onslaught of shadows

what I do is talk to in tiny little bits
in every moment of the day or night
and at the end of the road where what I do is to you
how wrong and how long the tomorrows
but there she is or used to be before this onslaught of shadows,
this swansway whalesroad where we were wishing
a boat to sail matchsticks down the rainfilled gutters
she betook herself to the places needful and presentable before
this whisper of shadows where the two men do what you can't see

## The smell of smoke

Some maintain their calm aplomb
despite the smell of smoke.
A train is moving in on her inexorably
like the train in the backyard
where we slept as children,
in a green house under a full moon
sitting straight up in our beds
in white cotton undershirts.
Some rattled ice in a glass.
Some walked slowly towards us as if
forgiveness could be held in a cup.
One woman recoiled from him
by smoking cigarette after cigarette
burned herself up sleeping in linen sheets.

## A conduit

She can't cry tears, can't work up a sweat
so you can't use any of those four letter words.
She simply doesn't get it.
no walls that give when smashed into, no all-day knees.
Sleep's a conduit, a way of trying it again.
Fruit came in little bowls, the word *gesundheit,*
candied cherries and syrup the color of pears.

## Stories

But such rupture between one's discourse and 'the place of one's experience' in the story of Philomela's rape characterizes other Ovidian stories as well.

And so the construed, the missing you and so forth longing parts of the story,
the tongueless parts
and the bird unable to say anything just to beat its wings against the glass
    you sit down
at the keyboard immediately.

The hermit thrush says it at breakfast, it's the hermit thrush.

The problem with the paintings is locale. It isn't mine, it isn't local enough,
no grapefruit in a bowl, no fingers peeling, the curl I saw in them both.

The portrait painting on the wall of the church shows a fraying head.

In the whole world, the fraying.

Pages plangent at the edges of their throats, at breakfast.

## The practice of going into the past

Since they both shared an interest in copying works of art
(the word *verso* in Italian means *toward* and *turn*)
dividing the canvas into equal quarters, setting up a grid from which
to walk toward or away from the exact location of where
they'd stood the last time when you
never were the same eyes she looks down out of.
Then you wonder why she always looks down and never out
although it's true the sun's too bright in this city
often compared to Italian cities for its light and shadows
you could pick up like cut-outs and lay out across stucco walls.
It isn't the same as it was before as she writes about the shift in size,
the unlikely stanzas she can't recover but by fits and starts.

## After the war

Black and white arches face one another in the year I was almost born.
The arch of one seems to mirror the arch of the other
conveying what appears to be a convincing spatial illusion revealing the ideal
as an artificial construction of disrupted perspective—
no vanishing lines to the place of origin where the mother is said to have said.
Logic and common sense only interfere.
Now there is no *after:* wars go on endlessly.
She remembers finding the newspaper in the basement moldy and damp.

## Not knowing the language

He took her to lessons she couldn't speak the language of,
just the noise of the train whistle in the distance.
A thread out of silence she had thought she'd have
someone to talk to if she could get him out, and what would it be
to talk to someone who would listen until you stopped talking.
But when she opens her mouth cold mountain air
rushes in and all she wants is to lie in the Mediterranean sun
and soak up a few more hours on the station clock.

## Newscasts

She practiced lying on one side
and when she turned over to talk to them
she remembered the awkward hip strain,
the flopping of inevitable feet.
If you stand in the sunlight and look in the arcade,
you remember the news of the nine-year old:
her brother beat her, her sister, her mother,
things pushed into the background with one system
and then another. The arches suggest reason
until the documents are other than you suspect
and even her own story seems mere story,
flickers across the screen.

## Dreaming of migratory birds

Sometimes you just know you can't live in that cubicle story, it's not
that you don't know cubicles, of course you do, but you know what I mean
they belong to someone else who is reprogramming and reentering
which you also do but you know what I mean. This is a story about time
and where the objects of the world locate or birds as they are
this afternoon. The man in the cubicle doesn't have birds in there
just memories of deserts and war. What I don't dream about is the birds
I wish I would dream about and how the world changes from country
to country under them as they migrate thousands of miles
as the woman throws her shoes on the floor to quiet their tinny cries.

## Compositions in other forms

Monteverdi set her to music in 1608 lamenting her abandonment.
An out-of-print recording, *Lamento d'Arianna* shows up on screen.
I like to think she made herself marble and set up in the town square
so that people passing could watch her sleep. *Lasciatemi morire.*
In 1901 Atget photographed the reclining statue from the side,
blank where there would be sky, blank where ground,
framed between two standing sculptures,
a visual rhyme between the rectangular base of the sculpture
and the squared-off topiary behind it.
It is very hot this July afternoon and very French and she will mistake the wind
and lie down thinking of a body she took out for Van Cleve.

## The idea of the body

The body is an idea someone might have had:
an idea that will strike her in another moment
at the location of her left eye
as they insist on the position of the body
in the corner, crouching and scratching.
She leans down and picks it up slowly, carefully,
and carries it into the room where they've gathered
and slips it between one person and another,
guiding it between them,
and she notices all the men have antlers
and she only manages to recover
by rearranging the idea of her body under the arcade
and in gathering up the edges of the shadow
as a cloak to cover her bare shoulders.

## What comes before

You walk into the night to remember who you were then
and you try to remember what it might be good to say
while saying all the things you remember about the city
because of the lights you saw in the rooms
where men in vests were watching TV
and his father looked out at him and cringed
and it made the story he was telling more about the intrusions
than the windows you were looking into
or you were crawling out over chipped paint
and into the alley you were that age almost fully
then you were in the window where the hastily moving curtains,
the proportions and the arc-like plumes of water
in the preliminary sketch weren't where you were then.

## *In the first place* is one way of beginning

In the photograph of the two there were always three,
someone was waiting outside the frame of overheated children.
I needed to take notes, to write down the characters,
to get hold of a cry coming out sooner than the name for it.
The first choice is the way of a headache
the edge of looking out the window is what I would write in the notes
if I were taking down what I was stepping on where the three of us
at the start of the page where there was a cry out of which
the initial character began, her mouth opening up.

## Having to

Even the pungent lilacs won't do it
nor elbows, the peculiar knot of multiple bones
for which I'm grateful and the hard certainty of the floor
almost always there. It must be time to open the door
knowing the hallway I've always known is waiting,
just to move what used to be feet in the dark,
voice long gone down some corridor mumbling a page
feet swung wide over the line so far it turns
onto the following indented and empty space
so familiar to those of us engaged in mythology.
Experience is only a slant rhyme,
boxwoods trimmed to simulate order in the high garden.

## The time the photograph was taken

In general the hands of the clocks indicate a far less advanced hour
than the length of shadows would suggest,
in general one tries for historical accuracy but
it can't account for the eye of the beholder.
It has only eleven numbers not only in the studio
but when she begged him to return with her
she couldn't get her voice up high enough
couldn't shape human conditions.
He kept reworking the composition with a luminous band of color.
She kept reworking the same events.
Her work was cut out for her though she tried to ignore the consequences.
But she never anticipated the fires of war,
merely squinted into the bright sun.

## *Hurry up please*

You wish you could go back to it all his plays are about that
and you see how vivid the places moved away from are,
how he stops by and lifts his fingers, one by one,
the argument at the back of your throat, moments ticking past.
Here's a new start without the haunted evenings,
the tree out the third floor window you leapt into
nights when all the houses slept.
The groveling and pushing back, the pages
turned and even names of the people you can't remember,
the vegetal and vegetation, all the feet on the stairs
when light erases all metaphor and the only moment connecting
this to that is, of course, what his plays are all about.

## Theatricality

She lies prone in a collapsed attitude, clutching her chest in a trance.
They now greet each other with gestures of reconciliation,
they now manage it by skirting the theater that lies somewhat buried
under *sedge* a word that won't materialize in a dry climate.
If you write for the theater, more can happen at this juncture,
lights can go up or the rattle of tinny thunder
as when he drove me to the airport and I knew I was leaving
and all the thinking in the world wouldn't stop
the plane from taking off or get back to yesterday.

It's hard to teach theater I said, the character takes on
an entirely different body in the second half and it would be hard
to imagine the scene without a flash from the light board.
On the way to the airport clutching the wheel one knows it's the last time
and no painting in the series will be the same and nothing that has
happened before will be a lesson to you in exactly the same way.

# Shakespearean Women

## Shakespeare's Cleopatra

*From the outset she knows her own death coming,*
*the soothsayer's as much as told her so*

*if it be not now/ yet it will come (Hamlet 5.2)*

plunging about the stage no matter what
slipping in and out of genders, dressing up,
pleading, leading, arranging herself
as if she were Venus in cloth of gold tissue, purple sails on her barge,

as if she could rise above the mortal even as she falls
into giddy play, refusing efforts to pin her down:

as if Egyptian queen, lascivious and astute,
over-the-top desired and desiring,
the mother of eight, also martial, also coy,

and performing her own dying at the end
as if she weren't, as she knows, already in the future
theater within theater

the frenetic shifting of who do you think I am

and couldn't we ourselves fret the edges,
revise what others say we are, we ordinary mortals

***

time's a vicious substance through which we pass

when I know I'm not in the future it comes round to me as queasy

who wants to listen to "we'll meet up again next year, perhaps,"
*perhaps* you'll see her again, *perhaps*

*I couldn't be happier to have known you*

aging or ageless, stepping perchance, that is, as if, into the Aegean Sea
    where Cycladic bodies of women
    of the FAF (folded arm figure) seem to circle around as if
        out of their Getty vitrines, naked, amused

blank-face, zoom face, flattened face, sculpted-face,
a creature this old sitting here
my face a flattened field, one sharp nose with bony outcropping

Cleopatra says she's winkled deep in time, yet
age can't wither her, potent and dissolving

asps on her arms

    raising the inevitable question whether reading ever makes for
kinship*

***

where's wisdom without one hand clasped by another,

lying down, a spine remembers we're put together in the same way—
    the bones therein

analogous, mirrored—yet analogy frets us
simple and crude yet we sense the need of it—some crossing over
    into text, body, image, age or ageless

    each brings all one's seen and read and birthed and loved
and listened to, each birdsong and evensong,
and long ago in a smoky room, Bartok's *Strings, Percussion and Celesta,*
the shoulderloads we carry, a diseased elm,
    uprooted from the corner yard, a swim, lopsided, a walk

    then a painting stops me dead in my tracks

---

* (all my life I've spent reading—does it extend whoever we are—
if only illusion, might illusion shape itself around another
might it impart a sense that each is more in many ways
not exactly visible, but nevertheless, embrace
the potential of the subjunctive)

people gliding their strokes of watery paint in that one
draperies fading out of view beyond the frame

they're between one world and the next
        an angle of slight perfume walking by

standing next to them staring at the sky, Venus rising,
clamber up some craggy hill, grieve with,

        a sister keeps spider webs on her windows so birds won't fly
                into the glassy reflection of trees

(myopia made it a matter of course, things always looked like
other things—were always *as if*, the unexpected reforming in front of my eyes)

***

"half blasted ere I knew you" Antony says, "I found you as a morsel,
cold upon dead Caesar's trencher"

        (one I loved just stopped eating and taking water and I never saw her again
        old and in pain, she just decided)
        (another was given drugs that didn't stop the pain, her skull
        so small in between my hands)

Cleopatra climbs onto her monument, speaks herself mythic
        how stagy she is, how hyperbolic in defeat,
                couldn't someone put words in my mouth

of course the playwright knows the myth but what she says
he gets to work out:

                *Husband I come:*
        *Now to that name, my courage prove my title!*
        *I am fire, and air; my other elements*

*I give to baser life.* *

twas a boy afterall an all-male cast, gender bending around all corners and comers
twas this twas that throughout a life in and out and able to hang upside down
on the treelimb   carry hay to the field   run faster than   and old   more
  likely to die
more likely to   Cleopatra hopping about girlish

aren't we allied to one another, what sort of person was she
who speaks to us over the years, and what did she think about
in her own skin mornings then, my mother, unknown

what ragged analogies open up despite their limits
whose body's being done to, in what ways in what imagined spaces
how many times the pain of it, she says you can't imagine
each spine moving in its own efforts, uncurling to the sky

    it's that I put my finger on belated as it is, it is always belated
    each spine moving on its own parallel to my own
    each image a revision

each revision a mirage— so

        in this desert imagine water, perhaps an abandoned sink
rivulets on elbows
    being done to by waterfalls   even a bucket could do it
    in discrete time   could we do with or without analogies

        the whole group of us   at the spigot

---

* She stages her death, positioning herself at the transition from one kind of morsel to another, from fleshly substance to allegory. The move towards allegory is daring, yet it does not and cannot obliterate the actual stage body of an obviously spectacular Cleopatra. In part, of course, this is what the boy actor must create in his performance. She is embodied by the actor, and he would draw special attention to the "maternal body" by the baring of the breast to nurse her baby, the asp "that sucks the nurse aslee." (Ronk, academic essay).

## Nobody (Desdemona and essential workers)

*In the English Public theater of Shakespeare's time no women were permitted to appear onstage. In the cross-dressing plays in which the heroine disguised herself as a boy, the boy actor would then be playing a girl playing the part of a boy.*

Nobody I'm nobody she says to the walls before she is
laid out like a woman laid out for everyone to stare at.
She is wearing a nightdress from a sweatshop by the *Kung Fu*.
It has frills at the neck and along the breasts he doesn't have.
She sings the song her maid Barbery taught her,
*sing willow, willow, all a green willow.*

*The willow emblem suggests her knowledge of herself--her subjectivity residing in an articulation of distance from herself–and of her cultural position as oppressed female. It is the very structure of allegory that designates subjectivity as simultaneously etched and unreadable.**

**The nightdress is made in multiple lots by women who travel by bus from east LA to the corner where they work behind a locked door and blackened windows. When you walk by you can hear salsa music, but you can't see anyone. Sometimes all the women of a family come together so mothers and sisters and children are all sewing together and talking together although it is difficult to hear anyone over the noise of the machines.**

*The use of the willow emblem achieves the uncanny effect of making the invisible appear visible; it produces an hallucination, or rather an hallucinatory effect*

The actor playing her is young and beardless and recently come to London.
He is lithe and graceful and plays women's roles easily.
Like his mother he has a lovely singing voice.

Nobody I'm nobody she says it to the walls waiting for Othello to suffocate her.
Then she lays herself out on the bed waiting.

*Another way in which she represents her own intense subjectivity, more problematic than the first, although bound up with it, is as one obliterated, as if whatever the rep-*

---

* Martha Ronk, "Desdemona's Self-Presentation," *English Literary Renaissance*, winter 2005.

*resentation of self might be, it must derive from nothingness, from being, as Desdemona says when she revives momentarily to speak her eerie lines, "Nobody."*

She lies down in a nightgown, dressed and undressed.
The women walk to the bus past the signs for kung fu and pizza,
inside are the silent songs in another tongue.

**The women from Guatemala pull their hair into barrettes and headbands and walk into the shop hand in hand telling stories of home as the young ones strut huddle at the side of the old ones who lose their voices past the threshold and find only their fingers and eyes and the nightgowns in polyester printed with the floating heads of red Santas looking out on the world.**

*She sheds her social role in order to represent herself more intimately and revealingly. By changing to a nightgown—the foreshadowing of death—she announces she knows she is to die. As Desdemona undresses, the undoing of her character is amplified by the undoing of the female disguise. The difficulty of maintaining the disguise and the role while removing the clothes necessary for such a disguise (and revealing what parts of the body aren't there) radically deconstructs character within the play and in the theater at large.*

## Dust/Daphne

one becoming the other noiselessly— the urn before it's smashed

into the ground, an incomplete memory holding wine,

prose so like poetry and Daphne herself into branches needing pruning

before the tree (a plum planted many years before on the property) can be seen

a mystery unfolding like Daphne herself, stick upon stick

what has become of her/
                                        of him :   as he wrote it, he being the "author"

and what shall we call it without its pedestal, without its color so faded with time,

blue symbolism absorbed by the clay itself, the clay itself become so fine

any wind could scatter it like dust so like the place itself where it was placed

many years before and will be again.

> *What is meant by Origin is not the becoming of something that has sprung forth, but rather what springs forth out of coming to be and passing away... The original never reveals itself in the bare and manifest existence of the factual.*
>
> —Walter Benjamin

## natural/unnatural

scrapping the mannered and hyper-corrected is a tactic &
others have done it perhaps with effort, who knows
or perhaps if their recall is spot-on or if the open books on the table
prod a "natural" response or

refer viz. to Simon Weil's discussion of dancing around the heavy stone,
bodies and levers figuring out movement together,

language being a refinement of sensation: *First there must be firm, hard stone*
*for building and the blocks are laid rough-hewn one on another.*
*Afterwards it's certainly important*
*that the stone can be trimmed, that it's not too hard.*

as Florizel sd in praising Perdita: when you do dance, *I'd wish you a wave o' the sea,*
*that you might ever do nothing but that, move so,*
*still so, and own no other function.*

sounding completely natural once you're used to it, once transplanted to the stage.

*Hello, This is she.* The once phone. Single phone. The once child. *This is she.*

And no one talks as Wayne did, saying the plants have their feet in water, the 19th century invading his prose via Wordsworth—
"O joy! that in our embers/ Is something that doth live,/ That nature yet remembers /
What was so fugitive"

although nothing in his garden is natural although it may look as if it is
although people may say so and think so, so it seems natural to me

although the weediness is deceiving

what does it mean not to find one's own voice,
out of another mouth my own lips moving and the skin teeth tongue
ventriloquizing someone else's for all time: *to be or not to be*

as all paths must lead somewhere: at the top of the ascent there might be a

terrace
cut into the hillside, backed by a retaining wall of dry stonework above and
within which
little alpines could be tucked, for the joke of suggesting that one had climbed above
the tree line to find tiny plants that reward the closest observation,

and then there are the voices one hears when there is no one there
and how artificial are those e.g. I read about the schizophrenic who learned
to check in with her co-workers and if they said, "no" to ignore
the messages the voices had brought that day

the oddity of languages one doesn't know speaking through the night
oil spills, nuclear waste, pathetic bickering in the Senate or what types itself
out on the page unplanned or finding oneself in the midst of wherever I'd
rather not

to have made it all up, whatever has been made,

but I know that others have done it, I read them and know them and hear them
and it is my dearest wish and even
excising metaphors such as white as a sheet, that duck or duck soup
or duck when you recognize the speed of it,

how much I miss the voices of those gone and when she sounds like her
how startled I am

still this can't be my own voice this one on the page, can't be

or has my years of a speaking crimped me up around the edges

so that nothing can be whatever voice I might have had but of course there was no
origin, innocence or other artificial backyard in which I spent those silent hours

the companions I was speaking to were the liminal friends
gathered with me on the stairs in the closet on the corner

when Beckett writes that the voice betrays the inner being, I'm amused,
struck by the sense of absurd connection like strings as when once you
know strings you can't unknow them

and besides typing isn't a voice

## Acknowledgments

This book is dedicated to my mother and sisters; and to women poets and Shakespeare scholars who have entered and remade my world through their texts. All my gratitude.

"De Chirico's paints" and "Lassitude of the Infinite 1913," FENCE 37-38 Spr-Sum 2021

### Translation of "L'ora inquietante"

All the houses are empty
Sucked up by the aspirator sky.
All the piazzas deserted.
All the pedestals widows.
The statues—migrated in long
stone caravans
towards faraway ports.
—Strange inscriptions crop up at each crossroads.
Gloomy warnings to *go no further*—

### Translation of "La Notte Misteriosa"

Two iron artichokes on the ocher table.
  The geometry of shadows lacerated the heart
    all melancholy morning.

### Sources

*Memoirs of My Life*, Giorgio De Chirico, trans. Margaret Crosland, Da Capo Press.
*Geometry of Shadows*, Giorgio De Chirico, trans. Stefania Heim, A Public Place.

## About the Author

Martha Ronk is the author of eleven books of poetry, including *Silences, Ocular Proof, Partially Kept, Transfer of Qualities* (long-listed for the National Book Award in poetry), *Vertigo* (a National Poetry Series selection), and *in a landscape of having to repeat* (PEN USA award). Her work has been included in the anthologies, *Lyric Postmodernism, American Hybrid, Not for Mothers Only, Exile—A Guide to Los Angeles Writing 1932-1998*, and others. Both her academic work and her poetry address the intersection of the verbal and visual and her work includes numerous ekphrastic poems. A collection of short fiction, *Glass Grapes and Other Stories,* was published in 2008. She has had residencies at Djerassi and MacDowell, and received an NEA award. She received a PhD from Yale University, taught at Occidental College, and published academic essays on Milton and Shakespeare.

## Free Verse Editions

Edited by Jon Thompson

*13 ways of happily* by Emily Carr
*& in Open, Marvel* by Felicia Zamora
*Alias* by Eric Pankey
*Ariadne, A Series* by Martha Ronk
*At Your Feet (A Teus Pés)* by Ana Cristina César, edited by Katrina Dodson, trans. by Brenda Hillman and Helen Hillman
*Bari's Love Song* by Kang Eun-Gyo, translated by Chung Eun-Gwi
*Between the Twilight and the Sky* by Jennie Neighbors
*Blood Orbits* by Ger Killeen
*The Bodies* by Christopher Sindt
*The Book of Isaac* by Aidan Semmens
*The Calling* by Bruce Bond
*Canticle of the Night Path* by Jennifer Atkinson
*Child in the Road* by Cindy Savett
*Civil Twilight* by Giles Goodland
*Condominium of the Flesh* by Valerio Magrelli, trans. by Clarissa Botsford
*Contrapuntal* by Christopher Kondrich
*Country Album* by James Capozzi
*Cry Baby Mystic* by Daniel Tiffany
*The Curiosities* by Brittany Perham
*Current* by Lisa Fishman
*Day In, Day Out* by Simon Smith
*Dear Reader* by Bruce Bond
*Dismantling the Angel* by Eric Pankey
*Divination Machine* by F. Daniel Rzicznek
*Elsewhere, That Small* by Monica Berlin
*Empire* by Tracy Zeman
*Erros* by Morgan Lucas Schuldt
*Fifteen Seconds without Sorrow* by Shim Bo-Seon, trans. by Chung Eun-Gwi and Brother Anthony of Taizé
*The Forever Notes* by Ethel Rackin
*The Flying House* by Dawn-Michelle Baude
*Ghost Letters* by Baba Badji
*Go On* by Ethel Rackin
*Here City* by Rick Snyder
*Instances: Selected Poems* by Jeongrye Choi, trans. by Brenda Hillman, Wayne de Fremery, & Jeongrye Choi
*Last Morning* by Simon Smith

*The Magnetic Brackets* by Jesús Losada, trans. by M. Smith & L. Ingelmo
*Man Praying* by Donald Platt
*A Map of Faring* by Peter Riley
*The Miraculous Courageous* by Josh Booton
*Mirrorforms* by Peter Kline
*No Shape Bends the River So Long* by Monica Berlin & Beth Marzoni
*North|Rock|Edge* by Susan Tichy
*Not into the Blossoms and Not into the Air* by Elizabeth Jacobson
*Overyellow,* by Nicolas Pesquès, translated by Cole Swensen
*Parallel Resting Places* by Laura Wetherington
*Physis* by Nicolas Pesquès, translated by Cole Swensen
*Pilgrimage Suites* by Derek Gromadzki
*Pilgrimly* by Siobhán Scarry
*Poems from above the Hill & Selected Work* by Ashur Etwebi, trans. by Brenda Hillman & Diallah Haidar
*The Prison Poems* by Miguel Hernández, trans. by Michael Smith
*Puppet Wardrobe* by Daniel Tiffany
*Quarry* by Carolyn Guinzio
*remanence* by Boyer Rickel
*Republic of Song* by Kelvin Corcoran
*Rumor* by Elizabeth Robinson
*Settlers* by F. Daniel Rzicznek
*Signs Following* by Ger Killeen
*Small Sillion* by Joshua McKinney
*Split the Crow* by Sarah Sousa
*Spine* by Carolyn Guinzio
*Spool* by Matthew Cooperman
*Strange Antlers* by Richard Jarrette
*Summoned* by Guillevic, trans. by Monique Chefdor & Stella Harvey
*Sunshine Wound* by L. S. Klatt
*System and Population* by Christopher Sindt
*These Beautiful Limits* by Thomas Lisk
*They Who Saw the Deep* by Geraldine Monk
*The Thinking Eye* by Jennifer Atkinson
*This History That Just Happened* by Hannah Craig
*An Unchanging Blue: Selected Poems 1962–1975* by Rolf Dieter Brinkmann, trans. by Mark Terrill
*Under the Quick* by Molly Bendall
*Verge* by Morgan Lucas Schuldt
*The Visible Woman* by Allison Funk
*The Wash* by Adam Clay

*We'll See* by Georges Godeau, trans. by Kathleen McGookey
*What Stillness Illuminated* by Yermiyahu Ahron Taub
*Winter Journey* [Viaggio d'inverno] by Attilio Bertolucci, trans. by Nicholas Benson
*Wonder Rooms* by Allison Funk

www.ingramcontent.com/pod-product-compliance
Ingram Content Group UK Ltd.
Pitfield, Milton Keynes, MK11 3LW, UK
UKHW041643190726
13854UKWH00006B/2657